SUICIDE

FORBIDDEN

**Casting All Your Care Upon
Him; For He Careth For You.
1 Peter:5:7**

By

Reverend T. Timothy

Table of Contents

Introduction

Self destruction is a main source of death. Self destruction is demise brought about by harming oneself with the plan to pass on. A self destruction endeavor is the point at which somebody hurts themselves with any goal to take their life, yet they don't kick the bucket because of their activities.

Many elements can build the gamble for self destruction or safeguard against it. Self destruction is associated with different types of injury and viciousness. For instance, individuals who have encountered brutality, including kid misuse, tormenting, or sexual savagery have a higher self destruction risk. Being associated with family and local area support and having simple admittance to medical services can diminish self-destructive contemplations and ways of behaving.

Self destruction is a serious general medical condition.
Self destruction rates expanded 30% between 2000-2018, and declined in 2019 and 2020. Self

destruction is a main source of death in the United States, with 45,979 deaths in 2020. This is around one passing like clockwork. The quantity of individuals who ponder or endeavor self destruction is much higher. In 2020, an expected 12.2 million American grown-ups genuinely contemplated self destruction, 3.2 million arranged a self destruction endeavor, and 1.2 million endeavored self destruction.

Self destruction influences all ages. In 2020, self destruction was among the main 9 driving reasons for death for individuals ages 10-64. Self destruction was the subsequent driving reason for death for individuals ages 10-14 and 25-34.

Self destruction and self destruction endeavors cause serious close to home, physical, and financial effects. Individuals who endeavor self destruction and endure may encounter serious wounds that can affect their wellbeing. They may likewise encounter melancholy and other emotional well-being concerns. Fortunately over 90% of individuals who endeavor self destruction and endure never proceed to kick the bucket by self destruction.

Self destruction and self destruction endeavors influence the wellbeing and prosperity of companions, friends and family, colleagues, and the local area. At the point when individuals kick the bucket by self destruction, their enduring loved ones might encounter shock, outrage, culpability, side effects of despondency or uneasiness, and may try and experience considerations of self destruction themselves.

The monetary cost of self destruction on society is additionally expensive. In 2019, self destruction and nonfatal self-hurt cost the country almost $490 billion in clinical expenses, work misfortune costs, worth of measurable life, and personal satisfaction costs.

Self destruction is the twelfth driving reason for death in the United States, as per the Centers for Disease Control and Prevention. It is characterized as the demonstration of committing suicide.

Much of the time self destruction happens with regards to a significant burdensome episode, however it might likewise happen because of a substance use or other issue. It now and again happens without any mental problem, particularly in unsound circumstances, like limit or delayed loss or declining wellbeing.

Note: *Suicide* or *Suicidal* is also known as *Self Destruction,* so don't be confused when you come across ***"Self Destruction"*** in the course of the reading.

Chapter 1

FOR WHAT REASON WOULD IT BE ADVISABLE FOR ME NOT END IT ALL?

Our hearts go out to the individuals who have contemplations of taking their own lives through self destruction. Assuming that that is you at the present time, it might talk about numerous feelings, like sensations of sadness and despondency. You might feel like you are in the most profound pit, and you uncertainty there is any desire for things improving. Nobody appears to mind or comprehend where you are coming from. Life simply isn't worth living...or is it?

On the off chance that you will take a couple of seconds to consider allowing God genuinely to be God in your life at the present time, He will demonstrate how huge He truly is, "in vain is unthinkable with God" (Luke 1:37). Maybe scars from past damages have brought about a staggering feeling of dismissal or surrender. That might prompt self indulgence, outrage, harshness, wrathful considerations, or unfortunate feelings of dread that have created issues in a portion of your most significant connections.

For what reason would it be advisable for you not end it all? Companion, regardless of how terrible things are a major part of your life, there is a God of affection who is sitting tight for you to allow Him to direct you through your passage of depression and out into His great light. He is your certain expectation. He is Jesus.

This Jesus, the immaculate Son of God, relates to you in your season of dismissal and embarrassment. The prophet Isaiah composed of Him in Isaiah 53:2-6, portraying Him as a "despised and rejected" man was "scorned and dismissed" by everybody. His life was loaded with distress and languishing. In any case, the distresses He bore were not His own; they were our own. He was punctured, injured, and squashed, all due to our wrongdoing. In view of His misery, our lives can be recovered and restored.

Companion, Jesus Christ got through this so you could have every one of your transgressions pardoned. Anything weight of culpability you convey, realize that He will pardon you assuming that you modestly get Him as your Savior. "...Call upon me in the difficult situation; I will convey you..." (Psalm 50:15). Nothing you have at any point done is not good enough for Jesus to excuse. A portion of His choicest workers carried out gross sins like homicide (Moses), murder and infidelity (King David), and physical and psychological mistreatment (the witness Paul). However they tracked down pardoning and another plentiful life in the Lord. "Consequently, in the event that anybody is in Christ, he is another creation; the old has gone, the new has come!" (2 Corinthians 5:17).

For what reason would it be advisable for you not end it all? Companion, God stands prepared to fix what is "broken," to be specific, the existence you have now, the existence you need to end by self destruction. In Isaiah 61:1-3, the prophet stated, "The LORD has blessed me to speak about uplifting news to poor people. He has sent me to tie up the beaten down, to broadcast opportunity for the hostages and delivery from dimness for the detainees, to declare the extended period of the Lord's approval... to comfort all who grieve, and accommodate the people who lament... to give to them a crown of excellence rather than remains, the oil of happiness as opposed to grieving, and a piece of clothing of commendation rather than a feeling of sadness."

Come to Jesus, and allow Him to reestablish your euphoria and helpfulness as you trust Him to start another work in your life. He vows to reestablish the delight you have lost and give you another soul to support you. Your wrecked heart is valuable to Him: "The penances of God are a messed up soul; a wrecked and remorseful heart, O God, you won't scorn" (Psalm 51:12, 15-17).

Will you acknowledge the Lord as your Savior and Shepherd? He will direct your considerations and steps — each day in turn — through His Word, the Bible. "I will train you and show you in the manner you ought to go; I will direct you and watch over you" (Psalm 32:8). "He will be the certain establishment for your times, a rich store of salvation and insight and information; the anxiety toward the LORD is the way in to this fortune"

(Isaiah 33:6). In Christ, you will in any case have battles, however you will presently have trust. He is "a companion who sticks nearer than a sibling" (Proverbs 18:24). May the finesse of the Lord Jesus accompany you in your hour of choice.

In the event that you want to trust Jesus Christ as your Savior, express these words in your heart to God: "God, I want you in my life. If it's not too much trouble, excuse me for all that I have done. I place my confidence in Jesus Christ and accept that He is my Savior. Kindly purify me, recuperate me, and reestablish my satisfaction throughout everyday life. Much obliged to You for Your adoration for myself and for Jesus' demise for my benefit."

WHAT DOES THE BIBLE SAY REGARDING SELF DESTRUCTION?

The Bible notices six explicit individuals who ended it all: Abimelech (Judges 9:54), Saul (1 Samuel 31:4), Saul's reinforcement conveyor (1 Samuel 31:4-6), Ahithophel (2 Samuel 17:23), Zimri (1 Kings 16:18), and Judas (Matthew 27:5). Five of these men were noted for their mischievousness (the special case is Saul's shield conveyor — nothing is said to describe his personality). Some think about Samson's passing an occurrence of self destruction, since he realized his activities would prompt his demise (Judges 16:26-31), yet Samson's objective was to kill Philistines, not himself.

The Bible perspectives self destruction as equivalent to kill, which is what it is — self-murder. God is the one in particular who is to choose when and how an individual ought to kick the bucket. We ought to say with the psalmist, "My times are in your grasp" (Psalm 31:15).

God is the provider of life. He gives, and He removes (Job 1:21). Self destruction, the taking of one's own life, is profane in light of the fact that it dismisses God's endowment of life. No man or lady ought to attempt to volunteer to end their own life.

Certain individuals in Scripture felt profound sadness throughout everyday life. Solomon, in his quest for joy, arrived where he "couldn't stand life" (Ecclesiastes 2:17). Elijah was unfortunate and discouraged and longed for death (1 Kings 19:4). Jonah was so furious at God that he wished to kick the bucket (Jonah 4:8). Indeed, even the messenger Paul and his minister colleagues at a certain point "were feeling the squeeze, a long way impossible for us to persevere, so we surrendered all expectations regarding life itself" (2 Corinthians 1:8).

Be that as it may, none of these men ended it all. Solomon figured out how to "dread God and keep his decrees, for this is the obligation of all humanity" (Ecclesiastes 12:13). Elijah was supported by a heavenly messenger, permitted to rest, and given another commission. Jonah got reprobation and reproach from God. That's what Paul discovered, albeit the tension he confronted was generally impossible for him to persevere, the Lord can bear all things: "This happened that we probably won't depend on ourselves however on God, who raises the dead" (2 Corinthians 1:9).

Thus, as indicated by the Bible, SUICIDE IS A SIN. It isn't the "best" sin — it is no more regrettable than different wrongs, as far as how God sees it, and it doesn't decide an individual's timeless fate. Notwithstanding, self destruction certainly lastingly affects those abandoned. The difficult scars left by self destruction don't mend without any problem. May God reward His elegance to every one who is confronting preliminaries today (Psalm 67:1). Also, may every one of us take trust in the commitment, "Every individual who approaches the name of the Lord will be saved" (Romans 10:13).

The self destruction of a devotee is proof that anybody can battle with depression and that our foe, Satan, is "a killer all along" (John 8:44). Self destruction is as yet a serious sin against God. As indicated by the Bible, self destruction is murder; it is never right. Christians are called to carry on with their lives for God, and the choice of when to kick the bucket is God's and God's separated from everyone else.

May God give beauty and the psalmist's point of view to every one who is confronting preliminaries today: "Why, my spirit, would you say you are sad? Why so upset inside me? Put your faith in God, for I will yet adulate him, my Savior and my God" (Psalm 43:5).

Self destruction is a frantic demonstration and a horrendous mishap for loved ones. What does the Bible say regarding self destruction and the destiny of the individuals who end it all?

What Does the Bible Say About Suicide?
A few religions instruct that self destruction is a reprehensible sin. Yet, what does the Bible say regarding self destruction?

Is self destruction a wrongdoing?
There can be no question that purposefully committing suicide is a transgression. The Sixth Commandment obviously states, "You will not kill" (Exodus 20:13), and self destruction is killing oneself.

However we ought not be speedy to denounce an individual who passes on thusly, for regularly, the person has been managing unquestionably profound issues. Those issues could incorporate some type of chronic drug use, including liquor abuse. They could incorporate at least one of various psychological illnesses, which can be hard to appreciate in any event, for the people who manage them expertly. What's more, the individual who ends it all frequently has been managing these issues furtively, the profundity of their battle known exclusively to oneself.

Does God excuse self destruction?

Could God censure somebody forever whose final venture is wrongdoing? We shouldn't dare to make a judgment around one's everlasting predetermination. Passing the last judgment is God's privilege, which He has appointed to Jesus Christ (John 5:22), not to us. Positively, we can make a judgment that self destruction is the incorrect method for managing one's concerns, however we ought to surrender timeless judgment to God.

Might God at any point expand leniency, even to their devotee life? All things considered, a devotee positively realizes that self destruction is off-base. Consider what the Psalms show about the personality of God: "For as the sky is high over the earth, so extraordinary is His kindness toward the people who dread Him" (Psalm 103:11). The Bible even weighs leniency against judgment, presuming that "benevolence wins over judgment" (James 2:13).

Fortunately, God passes judgment on every one of us on our whole Christian life, as opposed to upon a solitary mix-up.

Is there expectation for unbelievers who end it all to have post-existence?
Having considered the expected future for devotees who bite the dust by self destruction, what might be said about the people who don't trust in God who pass on thusly? Is there any expectation they will be resurrected once more? Indeed, there is.

Self destruction is stunning and has a horrendously horrendous impact upon the people who make due. Since that is the situation, some view self destruction as "an unpardonable sin." But it's anything but "a more terrible sin" than others. Endless individuals bite the dust without atoning of the many sins they have committed in the course of their life. What occurs after we pass on — including somebody who takes their life — in the event that we have not apologized for our wrongdoings?

The run of the mill suspicion that most Bible-accepting individuals make about the hereafter is that there are just two potential choices: that one goes quickly to one or the other paradise or damnation upon death. Truth be told, the Bible no place instructs that paradise is the prize of the saved or that an always consuming damnation is the predetermination of the denounced. Actually God has not completed the process of working with a great many people who have lived and passed on. Being the encapsulation of decency, He would not the slightest bit denounce somebody who passed on while never having figured out God's arrangement of salvation.

God doesn't censure anybody without first showing that individual how the person is supposed to live, without enabling that individual to comprehend, as well as the ability to satisfy His hopes. Indeed, even subsequent to changing over somebody, God keeps on working with that person, for all intents and purposes training and empowering any individual who has committed errors (and everybody does) to abandon them and back to the right pathway.

God has not yet done this with the vast majority who have at any point lived.

The desire for the revival

The manner in which God will work with these individuals is to resurrect them (to actual presence), so they could have their solitary opportunity at salvation. Permit us to rehash that point, so there will be no misjudge. This is certainly not another opportunity at salvation, yet rather the main opportunity for these individuals. In any case, don't take our assertion for this revival to genuine life. Believe God.

Think about this striking instruction from Christ. He discussed individuals who lived in various hundreds of years being resurrected and meeting on "the day of judgment" (Matthew 11:20-24; 12:41-42; Luke 10:12-15). Christ talked about the heathens of Sodom and the "fiendish" individuals of Tire, Sidon and Nineveh being resurrected with the sovereign of Sheba. He likewise told those conference His words at that point (in the principal century) that they would be resurrected alongside these others. There is just a single way this could occur — God should revive them together.

This isn't the very revival that will happen at the trumpet impact that reports the arrival of Jesus Christ to this world (1 Corinthians 15:52; 1 Thessalonians 4:16).

Rather, this is a subsequent restoration, which the Bible says will happen 1,000 years after Christ returns. The prescience of Revelation says that "the remainder of the dead" (the individuals who kicked the bucket without having gotten an opportunity at salvation) will "not live again until the thousand years were done" (Revelation 20:5).

Much justification for trust for the people who have thought of or serious self destruction
In synopsis, what does the Bible say regarding self destruction? It gives a lot of justification for trust about the fate of one who passes on by their own hand. We trust that the fact of the matter is ameliorating to our perusers who battle with the horrendous sorrow that main those near one who passes on by self destruction can be aware.

Chapter 2

WHAT DOES THE BIBLE SAY REGARDING DISCOURAGEMENT?

Sadness is an inescapable condition, influencing a great many individuals, Christians and non-Christians the same. Those experiencing sorrow can encounter extreme sensations of trouble, outrage, sadness, weariness, and various different side effects. They might start to feel futile and, surprisingly, self-destructive, losing interest in things and individuals that they once appreciated. Melancholy is frequently set off by life conditions, like a deficiency of work, passing of a friend or family member, separation, or mental issues like maltreatment or low confidence.

The Bible advises us to be overflowing with bliss and recognition (Philippians 4:4; Romans 15:11), so God evidently means for all of us to carry on with euphoric lives. This is difficult for somebody experiencing situational discouragement, yet it very well may be cured through God's gifts of supplication, Bible review and application, support gatherings, cooperation among devotees, admission, pardoning, and advising. We should put forth the cognizant attempt to not be caught up in ourselves, but rather to turn our endeavors outward. Sensations of discouragement can frequently be settled while those enduring with melancholy move the concentration from themselves to Christ and others.

Clinical melancholy is a state of being that should be analyzed by a doctor. It may not be brought about by sad life conditions, nor might the side effects at any point be lightened by one's own will. In opposition to what some in the Christian people group accept, clinical gloom isn't generally brought about by wrongdoing. Despondency can here and there be made by an actual problem that requirements be treated with medicine or potentially guiding. Obviously, God can fix any illness or turmoil. Be that as it may, at times, seeing a specialist for despondency is the same as seeing a specialist for a physical issue.

There are a few things that the people who experience the ill effects of wretchedness can do to ease their tension. They ought to ensure that they are remaining in the Word, in any event, when they don't feel like it. Feelings can steer us off track, yet God's Word stands firm and perpetual. We should keep up major areas of strength within God and hold considerably more firmly to Him when we go through preliminaries and allurements. The Bible lets us know that God won't ever permit allurements into our lives that are a lot for us to deal with (1 Corinthians 10:13). In spite of the fact that being discouraged isn't a transgression, one is as yet responsible for the reaction to the difficulty, including getting the expert necessary assistance. "Through Jesus, subsequently, let us consistently deal to God a penance of recognition — the product of lips that admit his name" (Hebrews 13:15).

What might I do for somebody who is self-destructive?

The danger of self destruction is alarming and ought to be viewed in a serious way. Commonly, such a danger is simply a sob for help. Those with self-destructive considerations might be troubled to such an extent that they can't envision life improving, and they basically believe that the aggravation should disappear. Self destruction might appear to be the main other option, yet its notice is much of the time a frantic endeavor to definitely stand out of somebody who might have the option to stop the aggravation.

Self destruction is sin, so anybody mulling over its requirements to recollect that (Matthew 5:21-22). Individuals are God's creation, and not a solitary one of us reserve the privilege to kill God's creation, regardless of whether we make ourselves the person in question. Self destruction is letting God know that He doesn't know He is doing and doesn't see how hard life is. Psalm 139:16 says that "every one of the days appointed for me were written in your book before one of them became." God sets the length of our lives, not us. Before we can help somebody who is self-destructive, we really want to have a reasonable understanding that self destruction is never a decent choice.

At the point when a companion or relative clues that he is mulling over self destruction, we ought to ask him to see a specialist. Commonly, gloom or some actual issue might be at the foundation of the self-destructive contemplations. Legitimate clinical treatment might mitigate the self-destructive contemplations and return the individual to sound reasoning. Doctors can likewise allude the self-destructive individual to an emotional well-being proficient for assessment and treatment. Drug and talk treatment have assisted many individuals with forsaking self-destructive considerations and returning to their lives. A concerned companion or relative ought to keep a nearby watch on the self-destructive individual to ensure she is completely finishing the ideas. Frequently self-destructive individuals couldn't care less about their own lives to seek after help, so adoring loved ones ought to step in and ensure the accessible assistance is used.

At the point when physical and emotional well-being have been tended to, we can help a self-destructive individual by likewise tending to his profound state. In the event that the individual doesn't maintain to follow Christ, her sadness could be because of an absence of trust or reason. A Christian can utilize this potential chance to impart Christ to a self-destructive individual. At the point when he comes to understand that his life has significance and his future is in God's grasp, the need to take his life might evaporate. Assuming that the Christian is uncertain how to make sense of their confidence, much assistance is accessible.

Some of the time the self-destructive individual is a Christian and has fallen into such a condition of sadness that God's commitments seem like fantasies. This individual likewise needs a clinical and emotional well-being assessment and the presence of a mindful companion or cherished one. In spite of our insight that what our self-destructive companion is mulling over is sin, this isn't an ideal opportunity to be critical. Nobody knows the profundity of agony and melancholy that another is encountering: "Every heart knows its own harshness" (Proverbs 14:10). Void maxims, for example, "encourage!" or "it isn't so awful" don't help. Frequently, the self-destructive Christian is agonizingly mindful of how wrong her craving is, which just adds to the despondency.

It might assist with understanding the individual, telling him that he isn't the only one to feel so low. Advise her that life comes in seasons, and she won't generally hurt this seriously. A new and better season is coming in the event that he can keep on strolling through this valley. Direct her to the hymns that express the profundities of human inclination. Peruse with him on the off chance that he is excessively dejected to peruse alone. Songs like Psalm 6, 42:11, and 22:1-2, which Jesus cited on the cross, help really put words to our heart's agony. Advise her that Jesus understands what such hopelessness feels like and He strolled through it for us (Matthew 26:38). The self-destructive individual isn't frustrating God because of feeling terrible. Any judgment is from the adversary, not God (Romans 8:1). We can delicately advise her that despondency is envisioning a future without God in it, and He guarantees never to leave us (Hebrews 13:5).

We should remember that, paying little mind to what choice a self-destructive individual makes, we are not liable for it. More often than not, loved ones fault themselves when somebody they love ends it all. This adds to the distress, yet the fault is lost. Friends and family might have taken a stab at all that they know to do, yet an official conclusion isn't theirs. On the off chance that it is not set in stone to end their life, there isn't anything anybody can say or do to forestall it. We are each considered liable for our own decisions. God doesn't consider us liable for the decisions of another. Bogus culpability is Satan's apparatus to take our bliss and future.

Chapter 3

SELF DESTRUCTION OVERVIEW

Self-destructive ideations are disturbing, yet help is accessible to stop them.

Self-destructive ideations are upsetting, however help is accessible to stop them.

Self destruction is deliberately acting to take one's life.

Self destruction endeavors might be arranged out or imprudent.

Murder-self destruction affects an individual killing another person, then, at that point, oneself. This is an exceptionally sensational, yet luckily uncommon, occasion.

Self destruction by cop affects an individual attempting to incite cops to kill oneself.

Self-mutilation is conscious self-hurt without a plan to take one's life. Self-mutilation is related with an expanded gamble of self destruction.

Most people who end it all have a psychological sickness like misery, bipolar confusion, or schizophrenia.

Diminished serotonin movement in the cerebrum is related with self destruction risk.

Individuals who feel irredeemable, vulnerable, or segregated are bound to consider or endeavor self destruction.

Individuals who have serious misfortunes - - passings of close individuals, loss of occupations, a move - - are more in danger of self destruction.

Like clockwork, some place on the planet, somebody closes their life.

In the U.S., around 100 individuals kick the bucket each day of self destruction.

Youngsters and more established grown-ups are bound to end it all.

Firearms are the most well-known technique for finished self destruction. Harming or going too far and suffocation/hanging are the following most normal strategies.

Individuals who have encountered tormenting, actual maltreatment, or sexual injury are more in danger of considering, endeavoring, or finishing self destruction.

Treatment of psychological wellness conditions can lessen the gamble of self destruction and work on personal satisfaction.

Self destruction is most just characterized as the demonstration of purposefully killing one's self. The word self destruction may likewise be utilized to depict an individual who has committed suicide. Self destruction is in many cases thought about as a no subject, and individuals frequently feel awkward examining it. This kind of disgrace may really keep people from letting others know when they are encountering self-destructive contemplations, and it might likewise keep individuals from getting some information about self-destructive considerations, in any event, when they might have concerns.

Contemplations of finishing an individual's own life, or of killing one's self, are otherwise called self-destructive considerations or self-destructive ideation. Certain individuals might design out self destruction endeavors, while others are hasty and at the time.

There are other explicit terms used to depict specific sorts or classifications of self destruction. Most suicides affect just a solitary individual. Once in a blue moon, gatherings, like individuals from a super strict group or religion, may end it all together - - a mass self destruction. An understanding between at least two individuals to end it all is a self destruction settlement. Albeit these are exceptional, they most frequently include a husband and spouse or other couple.

At the point when an individual first kills someone else (or people) and afterward closes their own life, it is known as a homicide of self destruction. The most widely recognized murder-self destruction is after a separation or separation, when one individual from the two or three kills the other and afterward oneself. Practically the culprits are all men (>90%). Considerably more seldom, an individual might kill numerous others prior to ending it all. These cases are extremely extraordinary (under 0.3 per 100,000 individuals; <3% of all suicides), but since of the sensational and horrendous misfortune around these occasions, they get a great deal of consideration and inclusion in the news and different media.

Self destruction by cop depicts what is happening when somebody carries out a wrongdoing or compromises somebody trying to drive cops to kill that person. It might very well be hard to be aware without a doubt what the individual planned when the person is shot by police. Also, a singular's self destruction in this way can significantly influence both the police required as well as the local area at large.

Willful extermination ought not be mistaken for self destruction. In willful extermination, somebody, normally a specialist, goes with a choice to take somebody's life effectively. Most frequently this is a patient with terminal sickness (a disease that will bring about death paying little mind to therapy) who has been considered to not be able to settle on their own choices. Willful extermination isn't lawful in the United States, however it is viewed as legitimate in a couple of European nations (Belgium, Luxembourg, the Netherlands). Conversely, the doctor who helped self destruction alludes to a specialist recommending explicit meds that are probably going to bring about death. Morally, doctor helped self destruction likewise requires an individual who can settle on their own choices, a specialist who will serve this job, and somebody who has a day to day existence. Moreover, self destruction (or "helped passing on") is unlawful in 46 of 50 states in the United States. Three states have regulations allowing self destruction (OR, VT, WA) and one state grants helped self destruction in light of a court administering (MT). Globally, the Netherlands, Belgium, Luxembourg, and Switzerland additionally permit self destruction. A more extensive conversation of the morals of willful extermination and helped demise is past the extent of this article.

Self-mutilation, like cutting, consuming, or scratching, is conscious self-hurt normally without planning to cause passing. Other normal strategies are raising a ruckus around town or different pieces of the body, squeezing, pulling hair, or picking skin. Although this normal way of behaving is generally not considered self-destructive (individuals typically say they aren't attempting to cause passing or serious mischief), individuals who self-hurt are bound to ultimately endeavor self destruction or even to take their lives by self destruction in the end.

Parasuicide, or parasuicidal conduct, is more hard to characterize. In a real sense, parasuicide signifies "like" or "close" self destruction. This could incorporate self destruction endeavors in which somebody makes due, self-mutilation, or self destruction endeavors in which the technique isn't supposed to cause passing.

Cautioning Signs Before a Suicide Attempt
Many individuals give cautioning indications or changes in conduct preceding a self destruction endeavor. While no particular way of behaving, or example of activities, can foresee a self destruction endeavor, it is essential to look for signs and ways of behaving that are disturbing. These admonition signs equal the gamble factors depicted previously. Changes or expansions in these ways of behaving are especially disturbing:

Expanded utilization of medications or liquor
Proclamations taking steps to damage or commit suicide
Talking or expounding on death or self destruction
Searching for admittance to guns, pills, or different means for ending it all
Articulations of sadness, purposelessness, vulnerability/feeling caught
Expanded outrage or fury, dangers of retribution
Expanded hazardous or careless way of behaving

Setting up a will or insurance contracts; offering significant individual possessions; making plans for effects, pets, and so on, to be really focused on.

After an extensive stretch of sadness and low energy, out of nowhere appears to be more splendid or ready to go

Any of these might be unsettling, however they are especially upsetting when they are matched with ongoing misfortunes, including passings, separations, work or monetary misfortunes, or clinical determinations. Assuming you see these admonition signs, it is basic to converse with the individual straightforwardly about any worries and get the person in question associated with assistance.

Self destruction Causes

This question is mind boggling and challenging to reply - - our best data comes from individuals who have endure self destruction endeavors or by attempting to comprehend what individuals who committed suicide might share practically speaking. On the other hand, certain individuals leave a self destruction note that might give some understanding into their perspective. Many individuals who endeavored self destruction show that they would fundamentally prefer not to bite the dust, however more frequently they need to end their aggravation - - close to home or physically.

The overwhelming majority who end it all have psychological sickness. This incorporates gloom, bipolar turmoil, nervousness, or schizophrenia. Furthermore, psychological sickness likewise incorporates substance-misuse issues. Substance-misuse issues incorporate liquor addiction (liquor reliance), liquor misuse (counting hitting the bottle hard), as well as reliance on or maltreatment of some other medication, for example, heroin, cocaine ("coke", "break"), methamphetamine ("meth"), sedatives/narcotics (oxycodone, hydrocodone, morphine, methadone), or others. At the point when individuals are utilizing liquor or medications (they are tanked, high, or stoned), they can be more incautious - - bound to act without contemplating what could occur. Sadly, this is frequently when self destruction endeavors happen.

Explicit side effects of psychological instability are connected with self destruction endeavors and finished self destruction. A sensation of sadness - - being not able to envision that things could improve

- - is normal in wretchedness and connected with self destruction endeavors. Individuals may likewise portray this as feeling caught or crazy - - this could possibly be connected with a psychological maladjustment. Here and there these sentiments can be expected to be harassed, mishandled, assaulted, or put through other injury. Defenselessness, a feeling that there is no hope to change things or to tackle their concerns, is likewise usually portrayed. Neuroscience analysts have attempted to comprehend what organic elements are connected to self destruction. Research on self destruction is intentionally attached to investigate sorrow, bipolar confusion, schizophrenia, and other psychological wellness problems with expanded chance of self destruction. The most grounded proof is connected to the serotonin framework in the cerebrum. Serotonin is a mind compound (synapse) that is engaged with temperament, nervousness, and impulsivity. Serotonin levels have been viewed as lower in the cerebrospinal liquid (CSF, or "spinal liquid") and mind of self destruction casualties. Synapses convey their messages in the mind by restricting to receptors, which are proteins on a nerve cell surface. A few kinds of serotonin receptors are likewise diminished.

Feelings of anxiety are additionally associated with self destruction rates. The body's reaction to push is directed by the hypothalamic-pituitary-adrenal (HPA) framework, a framework that connects part of the mind (nerve center) and portions of the endocrine (chemical) framework (pituitary and adrenal organs). Individuals who ended it all have been found to have unusually high action of this pressure enactment framework. Other cerebrum synthetics, designs, and movement have likewise shown potential connections to self destruction, yet the proof isn't areas of strength for as. There is even more that we don't comprehend about mind changes and self destruction, yet these discoveries guide us toward a path toward ideally better treating problems with expanded hazard of self destruction and to conceivably distinguish individuals in danger for self destruction sufficiently early to forestall endeavors.

Individuals who feel disengaged or different may go to self destruction endeavors as a departure. Individuals who have encountered sexual maltreatment or different sorts of injury are bound to endeavor self destruction. Essentially, veterans of the military, particularly the people who have served in battle or wartime, are at an expanded chance of self destruction.

Misfortune is likewise an explanation individuals think about self destruction. Misfortune could incorporate the passing of a companion, relative, or cherished one. Different triggers might incorporate a separation, loss of a heartfelt connection, a transition to somewhere else, loss of lodging, a deficiency of honor or status, or a deficiency of opportunity. It very well may be monetary misfortunes, for example, losing an employment, a house, or business. During seasons of financial issues (like the Great Depression or the new Great Recession), more individuals endeavor self destruction.

Assuming somebody near you ends it all, you might be bound to consider or endeavor self destruction yourself. Gatherings of suicides like this, particularly in teens or youngsters, are frequently alluded to as self destruction bunches or copycat suicides.

Certain strict convictions might impact individuals to end it all. A few religions might leave individuals feeling remorseful for things they have done and may persuade them to think they can't be excused. A few people might trust that forfeiting their lives (ending it all for their convictions) will procure them a prize (like going to paradise) or will be best for the religion. Certain individuals will end their own lives for their religion (saint themselves). Self destruction aircraft, frequently from outrageous Muslim gatherings, are an illustration of this.

In certain societies, for example, conventional Japan, disgrace or disrespect may be the motivation to take your life. This sort of self destruction, known as hara-kiri or seppuku, generally includes a particular function and custom blade.

Self Destruction Risk Factors

Despite the fact that self destruction is a moderately normal reason for passing, it is very hard to anticipate. Individuals who endeavor or end it all come from each race, country, age bunch, and other segment. There are many elements that are normal among individuals who kicked the bucket by self destruction, yet most others with these equivalent factors actually don't endeavor self destruction. For instance, despite the fact that the vast majority who end it all have some psychological problem, for example, sorrow, a great many people who have sadness don't end it all. All things considered, we can in any case find out about self destruction, and ideally improve at forestalling suicides, by understanding gamble factors.

Internationally, cultural and social factors additionally influence self destruction gambles. Networks with restricted admittance to medical care or that deter help-chasing conduct place individuals at higher gamble. Nations engaged with war or other vicious struggles, as well as catastrophic events, likewise will more often than not have higher self destruction rates. Ethnic gatherings who are confronting critical segregation, especially with dislodging or movement, are likewise in danger.

Certain segment factors are related with an expanded self-destruction risk, and since they can't be transformed, they are at times called non-modifiable gamble factors. These incorporate male orientation, Caucasian nationality, mature (under 25 or north of 65), and relationship status (separated, bereft, and single). Certain callings, like doctors and dental specialists, might be more in danger of self destruction. It isn't clear on the off chance that this is because of occupation stresses, information on and admittance to deadly means, or different elements. Joblessness or late employment cutback may likewise expand the gamble of self destruction endeavors. Critically, people with restricted social backings are at a higher gamble of endeavoring self destruction. People with a family background of finished self destruction are at higher gamble of self destruction themselves. This might be connected with inherited (hereditary) factors however may likewise be because of the injury and pain of losing a relative along these lines. Finally, one of the most grounded indicators of future self destruction endeavors is past self destruction endeavors.

Social variables, including current or past segregation, misuse, or injury likewise incline individuals toward self-destructive demonstrations. Individuals who have been liable to harassment are bound to consider or endeavor self destruction. This is valid both for youngsters at present being harassed, as well as grown-ups who were tormented when more youthful. Almost certainly, later strategies, for example, cyberbullying, would have a similar effect. A comparable example is seen for the individuals who have been physically mishandled or attacked, all kinds of people. For grown-ups physically manhandled as kids, self destruction endeavors were two to multiple times almost certain in ladies and four to multiple times more probable in men, contrasted with those not mishandled. Individuals who distinguish as lesbian, gay, sexually unbiased, or transsexual (LGBT) likewise appear to have higher paces of self destruction. Individuals presented to battle, either regular folks or military staff, have an expanded gamble of self destruction also. Albeit these stressors are totally different, they probably likewise affect individuals; individuals can feel secluded and vulnerable in controlling or getting away from these circumstances, and they may likewise feel all the more socially detached and unfit to connect for help.

A psychological well-being finding is one of the main gamble factors for self-destructive considerations or activities. Mental dissection concentrates on distinguishing at least one emotional well-being analyzed in 90% of individuals who finished self destruction. The most widely recognized analyzes are discouragement (counting bipolar wretchedness), schizophrenia, or liquor or medication reliance. The lifetime chance of self destruction for people with these judgments is higher than in everybody, despite the fact that reports fluctuate from around two to multiple times the gamble for everyone. People determined to have specific behavioral conditions, like solitary, fringe, or self involved behavioral conditions, additionally have a higher gamble of self-destructive considerations or ways of behaving. Liquor reliance expands the gamble of self destruction by half 70% contrasted with those without liquor abuse. Moreover, no less than 33% of suicides had liquor in their framework, 20.8% had sedatives (counting heroin, morphine or remedy pain relievers), and 23% had antidepressants. These measurements might uphold how normal sadness, liquor misuse, and chronic drug use are in the individuals who end it all, but a piece of this might be individuals involving these substances as a feature of their endeavor to take their lives. Albeit the relationship between a psychological instability finding and self destruction risk areas of strength for is, is vital to recollect that the vast majority with dysfunctional behavior don't endeavor or finish self destruction.

Notwithstanding formal psychological instability analysis, explicit side effects - - even without a full finding - - increment the gamble of self-destructive activities. Certain side effects of discouragement, especially sadness and anhedonia, are more intently attached to expanded self-destructive contemplations than a downturn finding. Sadness depicts an inclination that things can't change or be preferable over what they are presently. Anhedonia implies a failure to appreciate anything, or to feel intrigued by things that would typically give joy. Sensations of uneasiness (frequently additionally depicted as stress, apprehension, or dread) are likewise connected to self-destructive considerations. A few investigations recommend that sensations of nervousness or fomentation might increase that somebody is so prone to follow up on considerations of self destruction. An investigation of individuals who ended it all after release from a mental emergency clinic showed that 79% communicated "outrageous" or "serious" uneasiness, yet just 22% had self-destructive contemplations.

Issues with rest, like sleep deprivation, are an intense gamble for self destruction, whether they are essential for a burdensome episode. It is critical to take note that rest issues expanded the self destruction risk, even in the wake of controlling for different factors like orientation, mind-set, and liquor issues. Luckily, late investigations propose that overseeing rest issues can diminish self destruction risk.

Nonpsychiatric analyses may likewise build the gamble of self-destructive considerations and activities. A great many ailments, especially those related with long haul (ongoing) torment, a terminal (life-finishing) determination, or restricted treatment choices, have a higher gamble. A portion of the judgments displayed to have a higher gamble incorporate malignant growth, kidney disappointment, rheumatoid joint pain, epilepsy (seizure jumble), AIDS, and Huntington's sickness. Fitting treatment of these circumstances, and any simultaneous melancholy, can assist with working on personal satisfaction and diminish self destruction risk.

Defensive Factors Against Suicide
Notwithstanding the extensive variety of self destruction risk factors examined, there are likewise

factors that can be defensive against self destruction. Individuals who have great social backings, including relatives, companions, or different associations with others, have a lower chance of self destruction. Social gatherings that esteem family and local area connections and are affectionate will more often than not have less suicides. For people, having youngsters at home, and for ladies, an ongoing pregnancy, likewise are defensive variables. Strict and otherworldly practices and convictions - - including a conviction that self destruction is off-base - - can likewise diminish self destruction chances. Ultimately, keeping up with solid way of life propensities, including positive survival techniques, satisfactory rest, great eating regimen and exercise, can both keep up with and work on physical and psychological well-being, including self destruction risk.

Predominance of Suicides and Suicide Attempts
Like clockwork, some place on the planet, somebody closes their life. In 2012, there were 804,000 passings by self destruction universally, representing around half of all rough passings on the planet (1.4% of all passings). In 2010, for the U.S. alone, there were 38,364 detailed self destruction

passings (around 105 suicides day to day; one self destruction like clockwork). There are a bigger number of passings because of self destruction than murder (crime) consistently. A bigger number of men than ladies pass on from self destruction consistently, albeit the distinctions change by country. In the U.SThere are four times the number of men than ladies who complete self destruction, around 79% of all self destruction passes. In more unfortunate nations, the distinction in self destruction rates between sexual orientations is lower, with a proportion of around 1 1/2 men to each lady.

Despite the fact that self destruction may not be examined as much as different issues, including murder, malignant growth, HIV, war, and savagery, it is one of the most widely recognized reasons for death. In the U.S., self destruction is the tenth driving reason for death; a larger number of individuals commit suicide than pass on by murder (crime) or other savagery. Around the world, suicides represent a bigger number of passings than wars or murders.

Self destruction is more normal at particular ages: People in their teenagers and 20s, as well as more established grown-ups, are probably going to endeavor or finish self destruction. Self destruction is the third driving reason for death for individuals ages 15-24, and the subsequent driving reason for individuals ages 25-34. More seasoned men (>75 years old) have the most elevated self destruction rates (36 passes for every 100,000 men). In ladies, the self destruction rate is most noteworthy in those matured 45-54 (nine passings for each 100,000 ladies). As of late, a portion of these age designs have changed, with self destruction turning out to be more normal in other age gatherings. From 1999-2010, self destruction rates for moderately aged individuals (35-64) expanded by 28% (from 13.7 per 100,000 of every 1999 to 17.6 per 100,000 out of 2010).

Self destruction rates change among various racial and ethnic gatherings too; nonetheless, contrasts in social convictions, financial status, and family structure are definitely more perplexing than these numbers would recommend. Around the world, self destruction rates change significantly among nations and landmasses. In the U.S., migrants will generally have self destruction rates like their nation of origin. In the U.S., Caucasians and Native Americans have the most noteworthy age-changed paces of finished suicides (15.4 or 16.4 per 100,000), while African Americans, Hispanics, and Asian-Pacific Islanders have about a portion of this rate (5.5, 5.7, or 5.8 per 100,000).

There are a lot more self destruction endeavors than passes by self destruction. Since many endeavors are not detailed, gauges are probably lower than the real number. Most reports propose that for each self destruction, there are presumably somewhere around 20-25 self destruction endeavors. In individuals ages 15-24, there might be upwards of 100-200 individuals who make due for each finished self destruction. Another measurement that is hard to compute is the quantity of individuals who are enduring relatives, accomplices, or dear companions of each and every casualty of self destruction - - otherwise called overcomers of self destruction. A low gauge is that something like six individuals are genuinely impacted by each self destruction, and that implies there are around 230,000 new overcomers of self destruction in the U.S. consistently.

For each individual who endeavors or finishes self destruction, considerably more have serious considerations or plans of ending it all. At the point when gotten some information about self-destructive contemplations and activities in the year 2008-2009, a bigger number of than 8 million U.S. grown-ups (3.7% of the populace) detailed serious self-destructive contemplations, 2.5 million (1% of the populace) revealed making a self destruction arrangement, and 1.1 million (<0.5% of the populace) revealed a self destruction endeavor. Among more youthful individuals, more than 17% of secondary school understudies (youngsters in grades 9-12; 22.4% of females and 11.6% of guys) have truly thought about self destruction, 13.6% made an arrangement (16.9% of females and 10.3% of guys), and 8% (10.6% of females and 5.4% of guys) detailed a self destruction endeavor something like once in the previous year. Further, 2.7% of the young people surveyed had a serious self destruction endeavor that required treatment by a specialist or medical caretaker.

Techniques for Suicide

As a general rule, men are bound to utilize firearms, blades, or other rough means. Ladies are fairly bound to take an excess or another type of harming. This distinction in sexual orientation in strategies probably represents the higher self destruction finish rate in guys. Worldwide, restricted information is accessible about self destruction techniques. The most widely recognized implies in various nations are much of the time connected with what is available and are in some cases in view of provincial patterns. The most broad information on techniques is from the U.S. Habitats for Disease Control and Prevention (CDC) National Violent Death Reporting System.

By a wide margin, guns are the most well-known technique for self destruction passing. Over a portion of U.S. self destruction passes are from a self-caused discharge wound. Guns represented 57% of self destruction passes in men and 33% in ladies. It is assessed that 90% of self destruction endeavors with a gun are deadly. More U.S. weapon passings are a consequence of self destruction than crime (in 2009, 19,000 versus 11,500). Regions where weapon proprietorship is higher will generally have more firearm suicides. Around the world, major league salary nations other than the U.S. have a lot of lower weapon proprietorship, and self destruction with guns represents just 4.5% of all self destruction passes.

Passing by hanging and suffocation (25.6%) and harming (counting physician recommended drugs, road medications, toxins, and carbon monoxide; 16.3%) are the following most normal strategies. Harming is the most well-known technique for self destruction in ladies, representing 36.5% of passings. These three classes represent more than 90% of U.S. self destruction passes in all kinds of people. Other more uncommon strategies incorporate falls/hopping, engine vehicles, and cutting/wounding.

In different nations, different means are more normal. In some low-pay nations with a high level of provincial residents, self-harming with pesticides is a self destruction technique and is remembered to represent around 30% of all self destruction passes worldwide. Due to simple admittance to implies, hanging is likewise a typical technique in low-pay nations. In Hong Kong and China, where a significant part of the populace lives in tall structure condos, leaping off of high structures is a typical self destruction strategy. Utilization of charcoal flames for carbon monoxide harming has spread as a typical means in China, Hong Kong, and other Asian nations over the course of the last 10 years.

Assessing Suicide Risk

One of the most significant, yet additionally generally troublesome, errands that emotional wellness experts do consistently is the self destruction risk appraisal. Since self destruction is generally exceptional, even those with psychological maladjustment analyze, anticipating who might endeavor self destruction, and when, is astoundingly troublesome. We know from research, notwithstanding, that the vast majority who end it all will see a specialist or emotional wellness proficient inside the prior month they end their lives. Knowing this, we should keep on attempting to be better at distinguishing those in danger.

A few experts approach the self destruction evaluation by utilizing organized meetings or rating scales to survey risk. Dr. Aaron Beck created one of the previous apparatuses, the Scale of Suicidal Ideation (SSI). The SADPERSONS scale was not difficult to utilize and had genuinely far and wide acknowledgment. Nonetheless, late examination showed that the SADPERSONS scale was not a precise evaluation for risk. All the more as of late, the Columbia Suicide Severity Rating Scale (C-SSRS) has been utilized in various settings. Approved rating scales enjoy the benefit of being tried on many subjects and of giving a goal, frequently numeric score to use in deciding. Be that as it may, on the grounds that self destruction is a complicated and low-recurrence occasion, no scale can be totally precise. Clinicians should in any case depend on great clinical judgment and record for factors not surveyed in these scales.

A more extensive methodology, incorporating a definite clinical history alongside an organized meeting, gives a superior premise to choices about risk. Notwithstanding, pressures so that clinicians could see patients all the more rapidly can restrict how pragmatic this can be. One illustration of a meeting based approach, which can be adjusted to various clinical circumstances, is the Chronological Assessment of Suicide Events (the CASE approach). The objective of this approach is to get a point by point record of self-destructive contemplations, arrangements and endeavors, alongside current mental side effects to best make treatment proposals.

For essential consideration specialists, time is much more restricted and should likewise be utilized to address a scope of other clinical issues. Evaluating each persistent for self destruction risk is unfeasible and has been displayed to have restricted esteem in forestalling potential suicides. Current suggestions are to evaluate essential consideration patients for sorrow and tension, and by giving suitable treatment, self destruction chance might be decreased.

Medicines for Suicidal Thoughts or Behaviors
There are no medicines that explicitly stop self-destructive considerations. Be that as it may, for every person, distinguishing and treating any psychological maladjustment, and managing any stressors can lessen the gamble of self destruction. A few medicines for psychological maladjustment, including significant despondency and bipolar issue, have been displayed to diminish self destruction risk. Certain prescriptions have been displayed to decrease the gamble of self destruction. Lithium

(Eskalith, Lithobid), a temperament balancing out prescription utilized for bipolar confusion or significant wretchedness, has been displayed to diminish suicides related with gloom. Also, clozapine (Clozaril, FazaClo), an antipsychotic medicine, can diminish the gamble of self destruction in individuals with schizophrenia. It isn't clear assuming these meds decrease self destruction risk when used to treat individuals with different findings.

Interestingly, there have been worries that antidepressants really increment the gamble of self-destructive contemplations. The U.S, as a matter of fact. Food and Drug Administration (FDA) has required an admonition expressing that antidepressants might expand the gamble of self-destructive contemplations in youngsters, teenagers, and grown-ups in their 20s. There was no proof that these meds expanded self-destructive conduct in more established individuals. This caution depended on a survey of studies that proposed this increment. A few specialists and clinicians can't help contradicting this admonition and feel that not endorsing antidepressants has really expanded self-destructive considerations and endeavors, since less individuals are treated for gloom. Continuous examinations will ideally address these inquiries all the more plainly. Meanwhile, it is vital that individuals taking antidepressants are familiar with this gamble and are given data about how to find support assuming they have self-destructive considerations.

Individuals who much of the time have self-destructive contemplations might profit from explicit kinds of psychotherapy ("talk treatment" or guiding). Mental social treatment (CBT) addresses negative considerations and mental bends. Mental twists are ways that the psyche peruses things around us in an excessively pessimistic manner (for instance, on the off chance that somebody gets a basic remark from one individual, the individual accepts everybody contemplating them). By rehashed practice, individuals can figure out how to defeat these idea designs and diminish discouragement and self destruction risk. CBT has been displayed in many exploration studies to assist with further developing side effects of sadness and tension problems. Likewise, persuasive social treatment (DBT), a kind of treatment created to assist individuals with marginal behavioral conditions, likewise can decrease suicidality. DBT utilizes care and other adapting abilities to diminish rash and horrendous urges that can prompt self destruction endeavors.

Assisting Someone With Suicidal Thoughts

Take explanations about self destruction, needing to pass on or vanish, or even not having any desire to live, genuinely - - regardless of whether they are made in a kidding way. Make it a point to converse with somebody about self-destructive reasoning; discussing it doesn't prompt self destruction. Examining these contemplations is the most important phase in finding support, treatment, or security arranging.

Assist them with finding support. Energize or try to go with them to find support. Call a hotline, center, or psychological wellness facility.

Eliminate unsafe things from their ownership or home. Eliminating any firearms is especially significant. Most self destruction passes utilize a weapon, and most (90%) of self destruction endeavors with a firearm are deadly. Other unsafe things might incorporate razors, blades, and sharp items. Remedy and non-prescription meds ought to be gotten.

Stay away from liquor or different medications; these can increase hasty activities and self-destructive considerations. Liquor is a "depressant" since it can exacerbate wretchedness all alone. Right around one-fourth of self destruction casualties had liquor in their framework at their demise.

Practice techniques to "dial back." If individuals can occupy themselves, in any event, for a brief time frame, the most obviously terrible self-destructive contemplations might pass. This could include anything from reflection, profound breathing, paying attention to music, taking a walk, or being with a pet. With an accomplice, companion, or relative, talking or even being there might help.

On the off chance that somebody is as yet feeling self-destructive, it could be useful to remain with the individual or to assist with tracking down others to remain close by. This kind of help or self destruction watch can assist with protecting somebody until they can find support.

In the event that these systems are not working, get help now. Go to an emotional wellness place, a trauma center, or even call 911. Self destruction hotlines may likewise have the option to associate you to nearby assistance.

Keep in mind, find support - - it can improve.

Forestalling Suicides in the Community

Self destruction influences many individuals, youthful and old, in each nation and culture of the world. Very nearly 1,000,000 lives are lost consistently to self destruction, with no less than 10 million other self destruction endeavors, and 5-10 million individuals impacted by the self destruction demise of somebody near them. Self destruction stays one of the most successive reasons for death all over the planet. The effect of self destruction makes counteraction a significant general wellbeing need and has been recognized as vital by the World Health Organization (WHO), as well as public, state, and nearby offices.

Things to forestall self destruction are best finished on a singular level, such as looking for indications of self-destructive contemplations and conversing with those you know. Nonetheless, a few changes can be executed on the local area, state, and, surprisingly, public level:

Confine admittance to implies self destruction. If profoundly deadly things like pesticides, toxic substances, and guns are less accessible, numerous passes can be forestalled.

Further develop admittance to medical care, including psychological wellness therapy.

Instruct individuals about psychological sickness, substance misuse, and self destruction.

Work to lessen physical and sexual maltreatment. Advocate for lessening segregation in light of race, culture, orientation, or sexual direction. Offer help to weak people.

Battle shame against dysfunctional behavior and those experiencing its belongings.

Support those dispossessed by self destruction.

Instructions to Cope With the Loss of a Loved One to Suicide

Find a care group, like an overcomers of self destruction (SOS) bunch. It assists with realizing you are in good company.

Anguish is altogether different for everybody. Try not to feel like you must be on somebody's timetable or course of events. It could take more time than you (or others) figure it will.

Find support for yourself, especially assuming that you have side effects of misery or self-destructive considerations.

7 Suicide Myths

Fantasy: Discussing self destruction could empower it.

Truth: Many individuals stress over this, yet there is no proof to help this trepidation. It is critical to talk transparently about self destruction, both to find support on the off chance that you have self-destructive contemplations, and to get some information about self-destructive considerations in those near you. Without open conversations about self destruction, those enduring might keep on feeling detached, and are less inclined to get the assistance they require.

Legend: The main individuals who are self-destructive are the people who have mental issues.

Truth: Suicidal considerations and activities demonstrate outrageous misery and frequently sadness and despondency. While this might be essential for a psychological issue, it isn't consistent. Many individuals with psychological sickness never have self-destructive ways of behaving, and not all individuals who end it all have dysfunctional behavior.

Fantasy: Suicidal contemplations never disappear.

Truth: Increased contemplations or chance for self destruction can travel every which way as circumstances and side effects differ. Self-destructive considerations might return, however are not extremely durable, and self destruction isn't unavoidable.

Fantasy: A self-destructive not entirely set in stone to end their life.

Truth: People who have endured self destruction endeavors frequently express that they would have rather not died but instead didn't have any desire to continue living with the enduring they were feeling. They are much of the time conflicted about living or passing on. After an endeavor, certain individuals plainly show that they need to live on, and a great many people who endure an endeavor don't wind up taking their lives later. Admittance to help with flawless timing can forestall self destruction.

Fantasy: There is no advance notice for most suicides.

Truth: When thinking back, a great many people who ended it all gave a few indications in the things that they said or did a long time previously. A few suicides might be rash and not arranged out, yet the indications of misery, uneasiness, or substance misuse were available. It is vital to comprehend what the admonition signs are and pay special attention to them.

Fantasy: Individuals who talk about self destruction will not actually make it happen.

Truth: People who discuss self destruction might be connecting for help or backing. A great many people aren't happy discussing self destruction, so they could bring it up in a kidding or impromptu way. Notwithstanding, any notice of self destruction ought to be treated in a serious way and seen as a valuable chance to help. The vast majority examining self destruction are encountering gloom, tension, and sadness yet might not have any help or treatment.

Fantasy: Suicide endeavors are only a "sob for help" or a method for certainly standing out enough to be noticed.

Reality: Suicide endeavors, even "minor" ones that don't need serious clinical consideration, are an indication of outrageous misery. Self destruction endeavors ought to be viewed in a serious way and are motivation to evaluate and treat any continuous psychological well-being issues.

Chapter 4

FOR WHAT REASON DO PEOPLE COMMIT SUICIDE?

With regards to figuring out what causes self destruction, there are various motivations behind why somebody would need to end their own life. Nonetheless, a couple of driving causes frequently represent a greater part of suicides every year.

Despondency: The most widely recognized reason for self destruction, profound burdensome contemplations are commonly gone with a feeling of torment and a sensation of sadness about getting away from the aggravation. It's essential to discuss sadness regardless of how awkward, as this can make people experiencing this disease open up more and become certain enough to shout out about their agony.

Psychosis: Mental diseases have been known to cause self destruction through mental debilitation. Schizophrenia is a kind of psychosis that is frequently connected with self-destructive propensities. Internal voices will order if not practical people to commit self-hurt, and should be blessed to keep these voices from turning out to be excessively legitimate.

Sob For Help: A weep for help happens when a singular experiencing inner or close to home torment, either can't or doesn't ready others around them and will endeavor self destruction if all else fails. Now and again, these people will choose techniques they accept will not really hurt them, yet are regularly unfortunately deceived

Mishaps: Accidental self destruction is an extremely normal reason among more youthful teens and youthful grown-ups. This cause can be connected to substance use issues, and normally happens to those experiencing a fixation. The best protection against this cause is to look for detox treatment or substance use recuperation.

Social Isolation: Common in a wide range of old enough gatherings, social segregation makes people experience depression, a known driving reason for self destruction, particularly among men. Frequently, those encountering social disengagement experience issues communicating their sentiments to other people and approaching self-destructive considerations. Because of the apparent danger of confinement, a singular will turn to self destruction as a method for getting away.

TREATMENT AND PREVENTION

Overall, around 3,900 Canadians end their own lives consistently - this frequently surpasses the quantity of passings brought about by street mishaps. Albeit more ladies endeavor self destruction, around four fold the number of men as ladies pass on from their self destruction endeavor. The justification for this is that men by and large utilize more deadly means like guns, hanging, or suffocation (suffocation). Ladies frequently use drug excesses or suffocation, or they cut themselves. Guns are utilized in around 30% of all suicides. Of all passings that include guns, around 80% are assessed to be suicides.

Certain gatherings have excessively high self destruction rates contrasted with everyone:

youths - in Canada, self destruction represents 24% of all demise among individuals who are 15 to 24 years old
young fellows between the ages of 20 and 24
senior men beyond 80 years old
jail detainees, for whom self destruction is the main source of death
individuals of First Nations and Inuit plunge, who have self destruction rates 3 to multiple times more noteworthy than the public normal; this is much higher for teenagers 15 to 19 years of age, with self destruction happening up to multiple times more every now and again than for other Canadian young people
individuals with earlier chronicles of endeavored self destruction
Causes
While the reason for self destruction is obscure, some normal gamble factors include:

major mental sickness - specifically, state of mind problems (e.g., gloom, bipolar confusion, schizophrenia)
substance misuse (basically liquor misuse)
family background of self destruction
long haul troubles with associations with loved ones losing trust or the will to live
critical misfortunes in an individual's life, like the demise of a friend or family member, loss of a significant relationship, loss of business or confidence
agonizing profound or actual torment
Cautioning signs and hazard factors
An individual who is in danger of ending it all typically gives indications - whether deliberately or unknowingly - that something is off-base. Look out for:

indications of clinical despondency
withdrawal from loved ones
misery and sadness
apathy toward past exercises, or in what is happening around them
actual changes, for example, absence of energy, different rest designs, change in weight or hunger

loss of confidence, negative remarks about self-esteem

raising demise or self destruction in conversations or recorded as a hard copy

past self destruction endeavors

setting individual issues up, like offering assets, or having a squeezing interest in private wills or extra security

However many individuals considering self destruction appear to be miserable, some veil their sentiments with extreme energy. Disturbance, hyperactivity, and fretfulness might show a basic wretchedness that is being disguised.

Many individuals accept that despite the fact that an individual could discuss self destruction, they won't really make it happen. As a matter of fact, discussing self destruction is an admonition sign that the individual is at a more serious gamble. In the event that you become so wrecked by your concerns that self destruction turns into a thought, you should be viewed in a serious way.

Discussing self destruction implies that the expectation exists to end your own life - regardless of whether you really make it happen. Forswearing won't convey the intimidation of self destruction and can let you feel more be and in misery. In the event that you are having contemplations of self destruction, see your primary care physician or a guide for help.

Step By Step Instructions To Help

Feel free to talk about self destruction. Assuming you imagine that somebody you know is thinking about self destruction, raise the subject. Individuals are frequently feeling better to converse with someone about it. Perceiving their anguish assists with facilitating the trouble of worrying about the concern of agony alone. It is critical to pay attention to what someone needs to say without condemning their sentiments. Remember that having no potential open door to discuss how severely they feel will just cause an individual to feel more segregated.

You may some of the time stress that raising the subject of self destruction will give thoughts to a generally discouraged. person. In actuality, showing your anxiety gives an individual access to the trouble of realizing that someone is paying attention to them. Assuming that an individual truly is thinking about ending their own life, talking gives an outlet to serious, frequently overpowering sentiments.

Pose direct inquiries - staying away from the point might show that you don't treat an individual's statements in a serious enough way to ask. See whether self destruction has been thought of, and on the off chance that they have thought out how and when they believe should make it happen. The more subtleties that have been worked out, the more noteworthy the peril that somebody intends to end it all.

Self destruction endeavors are many times a sob for help. While self-destructive individuals are as yet alive, they might be holding out trust that they will track down the resources to adapt to their feelings. Ask anyone who is thinking about self destruction to seek the help and clinical or mental help that they need straightaway.

Crisis help

Quick help is accessible for individuals who are overpowered by agony and dejection and need someone to converse with. At the point when an individual is in trouble, phone directing, emergency lines, and self destruction hotlines offer a no-pressure setting in which to converse with a mindful and unknown guide. Phone hotlines are likewise valuable in the event that you are self-destructive, stressed over a companion and need to understand what you ought to do in a specific circumstance.

Neighborhood administrations are recorded in city or territorial telephone directories. You can likewise call registry help with certain areas for local area administration organizations. On the off chance that there is an issue breaking through to the telephone administration, don't surrender; either call once more or telephone an alternate help. Help is in many cases extremely not far off, and can give a self-destructive individual the additional time they need to reexamine their choices and conditions.

Assuming that you are desperately worried that someone is in a self-destructive state, attempt to get them to the crisis ward of a medical clinic. Clinical experts can most actually manage self-destructive propensities and guarantee that individuals get the consideration expected to remain alive.

People who have hit a profound absolute bottom frequently can't understand how to pull themselves back up. Connecting and tracking down help - either among loved ones, or in strict or social establishments - can furnish individuals with a few alleviation and new expectations in their lives.

Seeking treatment

At the point when self-destructive contemplations are welcomed by a prompt relational life altering situation, then remembering this occasion or chatting with a dear companion or relative might determine the emergency.

People considering self destruction ought to have an expert assessment by a family doctor or psychological wellness expert to think about any of the accompanying medicines:

continuous mental advising (e.g., psychotherapy, conjugal treatment)
clinical intercession (e.g., more forceful treatment of an aggravation disorder)

mental treatment (e.g., treatment of a temperament issue, substance misuse, or schizophrenia.

What To Do When You're Feeling Hopeless or Thinking About Suicide.

Once in a while we experience such a lot of torment, misfortune, or deadness that we begin to feel miserable — like there is no chance to get out of how we're feeling. At the point when we feel sad or overpowered, we might begin to have considerations of self destruction. Self-destructive considerations are impermanent, and with the right treatment and backing, you can conquer feeling self-destructive.

What Suicidal Thoughts Feel Like:
Self-destructive contemplations can go from passing considerations about death — like pondering "what does it seem like to kick the bucket?" — to explicit plans about self destruction — for instance, pondering how and when to take one's life. In any event, passing contemplations of self destruction are reason to worry, as they can deteriorate on the off chance that they are not tended to. Assuming that

you are battling with any of these sentiments or ways of behaving, the time has come to connect for help:

- Feeling separated from others or pulling out from loved ones.
- Feeling caught in a painful circumstance.
- Feeling like a weight to other people or reprimanding others that they would be better without you.
- Thinking, talking, or posting on the web about death or brutality.

What To Do On The Off Chance That Your Suicidal Feelings Get Worse.

In the event that you are now having self-destructive considerations, enormous life altering events or terrible occasions — like a demise in the family or getting laid off from a task — can make those sentiments become more extraordinary or more continuous. Assuming you feel like your self-destructive contemplations are deteriorating, here are a few admonition signs to pay special attention to:

Raising hazardous ways of behaving.
Driving carelessly, for example, driving impaired or driving without a safety belt.
Expanding medication or liquor use.
Participating in hazardous sex.
Beginning or heightening self-injury.
Changes in diet, either confining your eating or gorging.
Changes in rest designs, either dozing excessively or excessively little.
Extreme changes in temperament.
Encountering emotional episodes of outrageous pity, fury, or uneasiness.
Feeling expanded crabbiness or unsettling.
An unexpected change in conduct from fomented or furious to quiet or even happy. While it might appear as though an improvement, this can be an admonition signal for a self destruction endeavor since it can flag beings are "settled" with finishing life. Assuming you begin to feel as such, look for help right away.
In the event that you experience a misfortune or unexpected life altering event, or on the other hand

in the event that you experience any of these progressions in your state of mind or conduct, connect with your emotionally supportive network for help. In the event that you notice these ways of behaving in a companion or cherished one, check in with them, let them know what you've seen, and inquire as to whether they need assistance.

Ways To Oversee Suicidal Thoughts.

Self-destructive contemplations are transitory, and conquering them with the right treatment is conceivable. It is pivotal to look for help from prepared psychological wellness experts who can help you before your way of behaving raises to a self destruction endeavor. In the event that you don't know where to begin, begin with who, where, and how:

Who to contact for help: People who are battling with self-destructive considerations need areas of strength for an organization. Request help from companions, grown-ups you trust, and emotional wellness experts like a specialist, therapist, or school guide.

Step by step instructions to request help: Be immediate. Make statements like, "I'm having self-destructive considerations" or "I'm feeling self-destructive. I need to discuss it yet I don't know how."

When you have experts to assist you, together you can evaluate your dangers and foster a treatment plan.

Recognize the Source of Suicidal Thoughts
Finding the wellspring of self-destructive considerations or sentiments can be troublesome, and can in some cases raise other troublesome issues to manage. Along with a specialist or guide, have a go at asking yourself inquiries like:

"When is the first time I can recollect feelings like this?"

"Was there an occasion or change in my life before I began feeling like this?" Remember, large life altering events or horrendous accidents can exacerbate self-destructive sentiments. The power of these sentiments frequently die down over the long haul.

"Do I feel more regret after a specific trigger?" and "Is this 'trigger' an individual, an encounter, or a specific point?" These inquiries can assist you with sorting out some way to lessen pressure or keep away from specific circumstances that trigger self-destructive contemplations.

"Is there anything that causes me to feel improved or disregard my self-destructive considerations?" This question can assist you with investigating new survival techniques other than contemplations of self destruction.

Make a Contact List

Every individual who is wrestling with feeling self-destructive requirements is an encouraging group of people. Make a rundown of contact data for individuals who can give you various types of help, like a specialist, your folks, dear companions, or other believed grown-ups like a school guide.

Confine Your Means of Self-Injury and Suicide

While you are in treatment for self-destructive contemplations or ways of behaving, it is great to confine admittance to risky substances or devices that can be utilized to endeavor self destruction. On the off chance that you want assistance doing this, ask an individual you trust to eliminate or confine your admittance to things like blades, guns, or liquor. For drugs recommended to you by a specialist, ask somebody you trust to store prescriptions for you in a protected spot and to manage you taking your medicine.

Diminish Your Stress

When you have a superior thought of the stressors or triggers that make you have self-destructive contemplations, it means quite a bit to track down better approaches to diminish your pressure and adapt to gloomy sentiments. A few suggested ways are:

Keep a social timetable. Have customary exercises with individuals in your group of friends, similar to week after week calls, espresso dates, concentrate on gatherings, or gathering exercise classes.

Attempt another leisure activity. Imaginative leisure activities like composition, drawing, composing, or singing can assist you with communicating your sentiments in another manner.

Keep a diary. Utilize a diary to record your contemplations and sentiments, both the negative and positive.

Work out. Move your body for the sake of entertainment ways to deliver "lighthearted" synthetic substances. Make an effort not to pass judgment on your wellness level, simply find an approach to moving your body that is a good time for you (e.g., dance, walk, do a Youtube wellness video, or go to the rec center)

Practice care and reflection. Care reflections carry your regard for your breath and staying present and can assist with bringing down your uneasiness levels.

Invest energy outside. Walk or sit in nature (terraces, parks, green spaces).

Connect with your faculties. Zeroing in on what you can see, smell, taste, hear, and contact can assist you with remaining at the time. Take a gander at craftsmanship you believe is delightful, stand by listening to music you appreciate, use cleansers that smell lovely, snuggle with delicate squishy toys or covers, and keep your #1 snack is convenient.

Make an "adapting pack" you can use on troublesome days. Add food varieties and different things that give you solace. Add photographs of your companions and friends and family to check out and kind notes to yourself to understand when you are battling.

Ways to change Treatment if necessary

Looking for help for self-destructive considerations can feel like a consolation, yet it can likewise feel overwhelming. Treatment is a long interaction, and giving the treatment a lot of time is significant. Assuming you are in treatment and your self-destructive considerations aren't disappearing — or on the other hand in the event that they are deteriorating — it could be an ideal opportunity to make changes. With your emotional well-being and emotionally supportive network, you can start to speak the truth about your experience.

Be Honest and Ask Questions

You and your specialist or instructor both have a shared objective: to assist you with defeating your self-destructive contemplations. So assuming you are as yet encountering self-destructive considerations or feeling self-destructive, it's critical to tell your advisor, regardless of whether it feels terrifying or overpowering.

You can pose inquiries about your treatment. While a significant number of us don't believe our specialists should feel like they're not working effectively,``"speaking the truth about what's not working for you can assist them with putting you on an arrangement that might work better. Pose inquiries like:

"What might you add to my ongoing arrangement that could end up being useful to me to diminish these contemplations?"
"What do you believe is working? I consider [part of the treatment plan] useful, however I don't think [other parts of the plan] are helping me."
"According to your viewpoint, for what reason do you suppose my condition isn't getting to the next level?"
Think about Changing Therapists
After you converse with your specialist, in the event that you feel that they are not the most ideal best for you, think about rolling out an improvement. Finding another instructor or advisor can be troublesome to your treatment, and not generally a choice relying upon various variables, similar to cost and accessibility. In any case, various specialists have various strategies, and on the off chance that your ongoing treatment plan isn't helping, it could merit investigating those various techniques.

Consider Lifestyle Changes

There are various elements that impact psychological wellness. Notwithstanding treatment, take a gander at your work-out daily schedule, diet, dozing examples, and prescriptions. On the off chance that your treatment plan doesn't address these pieces of your life, widen the arrangement to incorporate them. Investigate how drugs could help by counseling a specialist who will survey prescription choices, converse with you about secondary effects, and evaluate medicine choices.

Instructions To Help A Friend Who Is Feeling Suicidal.

On the off chance that you are worried that a companion is having considerations of self destruction however you couldn't say whether they are making substantial arrangements, tranquilly and straightforwardly express your anxiety. Ask them something like, "I've seen that you're going through a truly tough time. I'm worried that you might be thinking about self destruction. Are you having self-destructive considerations or feeling self-destructive?" This might be a troublesome discussion to have, yet it's significant. Also, it is vital to comprehend that examination plainly shows that getting some information about self destruction doesn't move self-destructive contemplations.

Assuming a companion trusts in you that they are having considerations of self destruction or are wanting to endeavor self destruction, there are a few different ways you can help:

Be steady, not critical. Disgracing or passing judgment on your companion's contemplations, or attempting to persuade them that self destruction is "awful" or "unethical," may exacerbate them. They might separate themselves further, which makes it harder to find support.
Urge them to look for help from a parent, specialist, specialist, or life coach. In the event that they don't have any idea who to converse with, urge them to call the crisis line for a free and classified discussion whenever.

Try not to vow to stay quiet about it. Assuming your companion is feeling self-destructive, they might feel like they need to stay quiet about it — however that keeps them from getting the assistance they require. In the event that they tell you, let them in on what you really want to tell a confided in grown-up for their own wellbeing. Urge them to tell somebody themselves.

Assist them with connecting for help. For instance, on the off chance that you're ready to, propose to assist them with tracking down a specialist or go with them to their most memorable arrangement. Proposing to be available for them during a troublesome time for them can be very supportive.

Urge them to avoid adjusting to substances like liquor and medications. Utilizing substances foolishly can be an indication that somebody is moving from self-destructive contemplations to self-destructive ways of behaving.

In the event that you have a good sense of reassurance doing as such, eliminate perilous things like blades, guns, or drugs not recommended by a specialist that your companion could use to endeavor self destruction.

Chapter 5

FIVE STEPS TO OVERCOMING SUICIDAL THOUGHTS

The following are five hints towards beating self-destructive contemplations that can assist with moving you away from harming yourself and towards recuperation.

Self-destructive contemplations can be truly challenging to manage or comprehend. Here and there they can be temporary, however different times they can be more grounded inclinations and dreams that guarantee alleviation from apparently excruciating torment.

Regardless of whether you figure you will not at any point follow up on them, all self-destructive contemplations should be viewed in a serious way - the earlier you can address them the better.

However it may be hard to stay confident, there are ways of defeating self-destructive considerations.

Here are a few hints to retaliate against considerations about taking your life as they occur.

1. Eliminate Yourself From Danger

Considerations of self destruction can hit hardest when you're in a possibly risky region or circumstance (hanging tight for a skytrain, driving, remaining in a gallery, or close to firearms, weapons, or other possibly unsafe items).

If so, actually eliminate yourself from the area or circumstance to limit the capability of following up on self-destructive considerations.

You can likewise ask a confidant companion or relative to take care of possibly hurtful instruments (e.g., weapons, rope) so you don't need to go close to them, or clutch any additional drugs until you want them.

2. Slow Your Breathing

Self-destructive considerations can be alarming, and it's not difficult to get overpowered. Easing back your breathing diminishes your pulse, while likewise moving your consideration away from anything that contemplations you're having.

Take a couple of profound breaths in and breathe out to recapture control of your breath - four seconds in, hold for four, four seconds out, hold for four - rehash. Assuming four seconds is excessively lengthy, begin more limited and attempt to move gradually up.

3. Re-focus Your Attention

There are numerous ways of doing this and some will turn out preferable for you over others. The objective is to pursue moving your consideration away from the negative contemplations of harming yourself onto something different. It very well may be extreme right away, yet the more you practice the more you'll have the option to limit any association with these undesirable considerations.

A. Representations

Zeroing in on breathing can help, particularly when joined with representations. Envision your lungs topping off with air, your stomach rising and falling. The more detail you add, the better.

Assuming you are counting your breaths, you can likewise attempt to envision working out the numbers - 1,2,3,4... 1,2,3,4...

For some purposes, envisioning yourself in a safe and quieting space, being with somebody you love, or shifting focus over to your confidence can help.

B. Utilize Your Senses

Shut your eyes for a couple of seconds and afterward open them. Concentrate on whatever is around you.

Have a go at portraying what you see in however much detail as could reasonably be expected - what's the surface of the ground, what tones are on the walls, what sounds might you at any point hear? Envision you're composing a scene in a book and be pretty much as point by point as could really be expected.

The more detects you use, the more you will actually want to move your concentrate away from excruciating contemplations.

C. Muscle Relaxations

Frequently, when you feel overpowered your muscles fix without acknowledging it. (Your shoulders or jaw might flex, or you might grasp your hands into clenched hands).

Center around loosening up your muscles. Begin with your head and gradually attempt to loosen up each muscle bunch working your direction down (face, jaw, neck, shoulders, back, arms, legs, calves, and so on).
You can involve your hands to rub your neck or shoulders too.

4. Connect

Notwithstanding the means above, connecting is critical. Regardless of whether you think the considerations are that serious, discussing them with others is a significant stage to tending to and removing the force of these contemplations. Encircle yourself with individuals you care about, instead of closing down and segregating yourself. For individuals to help - you need to tell them going on.

Call a healthline or a companion and clear up for them that you're going through an especially unpleasant time and need their help.

Loved ones frequently visit individuals as they recuperate from diseases like malignant growth or after medical procedures. A similar kind of help can assist you with recuperation from gloom. Perhaps a companion could come get you or remain with you that day or night. More on the most proficient method to reach a companion.

Try not to let stresses or fears of being 'secured' keep you from connecting and imparting your self-destructive contemplations to other people. There are various expert administrations and levels of care that can help, including finding and conversing with a specialist. Like treating different diseases or wounds, for certain folks clinic care is an essential and transitory step required for recuperation.

Assuming you want more pressing help, make it a point to 911. Your security is your main goal and there are experts out there who need to help. More on the best way to connect in an emergency.

5. Help Yourself To Remember Recovery

Part of recuperating from discouragement is figuring out how to beat these kinds of considerations and sentiments, without getting additionally stalled on yourself for having them.

Advise yourself that recuperation is conceivable. Numerous men have had comparable considerations and sentiments about self destruction, and made due - even men who have attempted to end their lives on various occasions have had the option to recuperate.

Having self-destructive contemplations can be disturbing, yet they truly do disappear. Attempt to sort out the best techniques for you, so you can endure any hardship.

HOW THE 5 STEPS CAN HELP SOMEONE WHO IS SUICIDAL

The five activity ventures for speaking with somebody who might be self-destructive are upheld by proof in the field of self destruction anticipation.

INQUIRE

How - Asking the inquiry "Are you contemplating self destruction?" imparts that you're available to talking about self destruction in a non-critical and strong manner. Asking here, impartially, can open the entryway for powerful discourse about their close to home agony and can permit everybody to be the one to ask the graphics involved to see what subsequent stages should be taken. Different inquiries you can pose incorporate, "How would you hurt?" and "What might I do?" Do not at any point vow to stay quiet about their viewpoints of self destruction.

The other side of the "Inquire" step is to "Tune in." Make sure you view their responses in a serious way and not to overlook them, particularly in the event that they demonstrate they are encountering contemplations of self destruction. Paying attention to their purposes behind being in such profound agony, as well as tuning in for any potential reasons they need to keep on remaining alive, are both unimaginably significant when they are letting you know what's happening. Assist them with zeroing in on their purposes behind living and try not to attempt to force your purposes behind them to remain alive.

Why - Studies show that inquiring as to whether they are self-destructive doesn't increment suicides or self-destructive considerations. Truth be told, studies recommend the inverse: discoveries propose recognizing and discussing self destruction may as a matter of fact lessen as opposed to increment self-destructive ideation.

BE THERE

How - This could mean being actually present for somebody, talking with them on the telephone when you can, or whatever other way that shows support for the individual in danger. A significant part of this step is to ensure you completely finish the manners by which you say you'll have the option to help the individual - realistically be the one to be there and don't focus on anything you are not willing or ready to achieve. On the off chance that you can't be truly present with somebody with considerations of self destruction, talk with them to foster a few thoughts for other people who could possibly help too (once more, just other people who are willing, capable, and suitable to be there). Listening is again vital during this step - figure out what and who they accept will be the best wellsprings of help.

Why - Being there for somebody with contemplations of self destruction is life-saving. Expanding somebody's connectedness to other people and restricting their disconnection (both in the short and long haul) has demonstrated to be a defensive element against self destruction. Thomas Joiner's Interpersonal-Psychological Theory of Suicide features connectedness as one of its fundamental parts - explicitly, a low feeling of having a place. At the point when somebody encounters this state, matched with apparent burdensomeness (ostensibly attached to "connectedness" through secluding ways of behaving and absence of a feeling of direction) and procured capacity (a brought down feeling of dread toward death and adjusted encounters of brutality), their gamble can turn out to be seriously raised.

In the Three-Step Theory (or all the more regularly known as the Ideation-to-Action Framework), David Klonsky and Alexis May likewise hypothesize that "connectedness" is a critical defensive variable, against self destruction in general, yet as far as the heightening of considerations of self destruction to activity. Their examination has likewise shown connectedness goes about as a cushion against sadness and mental torment.

By "being there," we get an opportunity to lighten or kill a portion of these critical variables.

PROTECT THEM

How - First of all, it's really great for everybody to be in total agreement. After the "Inquire" step, and you've decided self destruction is for sure being discussed, it means a lot to figure out a couple of things to lay out prompt security. Have they previously effectively attempt to commit suicide prior to conversing with you? Does the individual encountering contemplations of self destruction know how they could commit suicide? Do they have a graphic to guard them explicitly, point by point plan? What's the timing for their arrangement? What kind of access do they have to their arranged technique?

Why - Knowing the responses to every one of these inquiries can see us a great deal about the approach and seriousness of peril the individual is in. For example, the more advances and bits of an arrangement that are set up, the higher their seriousness of hazard and their capacity to sanction their arrangement may be. Or on the other hand in the event that they have quick admittance to a gun and are intense about endeavoring self destruction, then additional means (like calling for crisis help or driving them to a crisis division) may be important. The Lifeline can constantly go about as an asset during these minutes too on the off chance that you're not completely certain what to do straightaway.

A Public Health school noticed that diminishing a self-destructive individual's admittance to exceptionally deadly means (or picked technique for a self destruction endeavor) is a significant piece of self destruction counteraction. Various investigations have shown that when deadly means are made less free or less dangerous, self destruction rates by that technique decline, and oftentimes self destruction rates generally speaking downfall. Research additionally shows that "strategy replacement" or picking an other technique when the first technique is limited, much of the time doesn't occur. The legend "If somebody truly has any desire to commit suicide, they'll figure out how to make it happen" frequently doesn't turn out as expected in the event that proper wellbeing measures are established. The Keep Them Safe step is truly about showing support for somebody during the times when they have considerations of self destruction by investing energy and distance between the individual and their picked technique, particularly strategies that have shown higher lethality (like guns and drugs).

ASSIST THEM WITH ASSOCIATING

How - Helping somebody with considerations of self destruction interface with continuous backings can assist them with laying out a wellbeing net for those minutes they end up in an emergency. Extra parts of a security net may be interfacing them with supports and assets in their networks. Investigate a portion of these potential backings with them - would they say they are as of now seeing a psychological realistic be the one to help them connecthealth proficient? Have they before? Is this a possibility for them right now? Are there other emotional wellness assets locally that can actually help?

One method for beginning assisting them with tracking down ways of interfacing is to work with them to foster a security plan. This can incorporate ways for them to recognize assuming they begin to encounter critical, extreme considerations of self destruction alongside what to do in those emergency minutes. A wellbeing plan can likewise incorporate a rundown of people to contact when an emergency happens.

Why - Impact of Applied Suicide Intervention Skills Training on the National Suicide Prevention Lifeline found that people that called the National Suicide

Prevention Lifeline were altogether bound to feel less discouraged, less self-destructive, not so much wrecked, but rather more confident toward the finish of calls dealt with by Applied Suicide Intervention Skills Training-prepared advocates. These enhancements were connected to ASIST-related guide mediations, including tuning in without judgment, investigating purposes behind living and making an organization of help.

FOLLOW UP

How - After your underlying contact with an individual encountering considerations of self destruction, and after you've associated them with the prompt emotionally supportive networks they need, make a point to circle back to them to perceive how they're doing. Leave a message, send a message, or call them. The subsequent step is an extraordinarily realistic one to follow uptime to check in with them to check whether there is more you are equipped for assisting with or on the other hand in the event that there are things you've said you would do and haven't yet gotten the opportunity to finish for the individual.

Why - This kind of contact can keep on expanding their sensations of connectedness and offer your continuous help. There is proof that even a straightforward type of connection, such as sending a mindful postcard, might possibly lessen their gamble for self destruction.

Studies have shown a decrease in the quantity of passings by self destruction while following up was implied with high gamble populaces after they were released from intense consideration administrations. Studies have additionally shown that short, minimal expense intercession and strong, progressing contact might be a significant piece of self destruction counteraction.

Conclusion

SECTIONS FOR SUICIDE AND SUICIDAL THOUGHTS

Self destruction, ending your own life, is a heartbreaking response to unpleasant life circumstances — and even more shocking on the grounds that self destruction can be forestalled. Whether you're thinking about self destruction or know somebody who feels self-destructive, learn self destruction cautioning signs and how to connect for guaranteed help and expert treatment. You might save a day to day existence — your own or another person's.

Discussing self destruction — for instance, offering expressions, for example, "I will commit suicide," "I want to be dead" or "I wish I wasn't conceived" Getting the resources to end your own life, like purchasing a firearm or storing pills

Pulling out from social contact and needing to be let be

Having emotional episodes, for example, being genuinely high one day and profoundly deterred the following.

Being distracted with death, passing on or brutality

Having a caught or irredeemable outlook on a circumstance

Expanding utilization of liquor or medications

Changing typical daily schedule, including eating or dozing designs

Doing hazardous or foolish things, like utilizing medications or driving wildly

Offering effects or getting undertakings all together when there could be not an obvious reason for doing this

Expressing farewell to individuals as though they will not be seen in the future

Creating character changes or being seriously restless or unsettled, especially while encountering a portion of the advance notice signs recorded previously

Cautioning signs aren't generally self-evident, and they might differ from one individual to another. Certain individuals make their expectations understood, while others keep quiet.

When to see a specialist

Assuming you're feeling self-destructive, yet you're not promptly considering harming yourself:

Contact a dear companion or cherished one — despite the fact that discussing your feelings might be hard

Contact a priest, otherworldly pioneer or somebody in your confidence local area

Call a self destruction hotline

Make a meeting with your PCP, other medical services supplier or a psychological well-being proficient

Self-destructive reasoning gets worse all alone — so find support.

Demand an Appointment

Causes

Self-destructive contemplations have many causes. Most frequently, self-destructive considerations are the consequence of feeling like you can't adapt when you're confronted with what is by all accounts a staggering life circumstance. On the off chance that you don't have trust for the future, you may erroneously think self destruction is an answer. You might encounter a kind of limited focus, where in an emergency you accept self destruction is the main way out.

There likewise might be a hereditary connection to self destruction. Individuals who complete self destruction or who have self-destructive contemplations or conduct are bound to have a family background of self destruction.

Risk factors
Although self destruction is more continuous for ladies, men are more probable than ladies to finish self destruction since they ordinarily utilize more-deadly strategies, like a gun.

You might be in danger of self destruction on the off chance that you:

Endeavored self destruction previously
Feel sad, useless, fomented, socially disengaged or forlorn
Experience a distressing life altering situation, like the passing of a friend or family member, military help, a separation, or monetary or legitimate issues

Have a substance misuse issue — liquor and illicit drug use can demolish considerations of self destruction and cause you to feel crazy or hasty enough to follow up on your viewpoints

Have self-destructive contemplations and approach guns in your home

Have a basic mental problem, for example, significant sorrow, post-horrible pressure issue or bipolar issue

Have a family background of mental problems, substance misuse, self destruction, or brutality, including physical or sexual maltreatment

Have an ailment that can be connected to melancholy and self-destructive reasoning, like ongoing infection, constant agony or terminal sickness

Are lesbian, gay, sexually unbiased or transsexual with an unsupportive family or in a threatening climate

Youngsters and teens

Self destruction in youngsters and teens can follow upsetting life altering situations. What a youngster sees as serious and unrealistic may appear to be minor to a grown-up — like issues in school or the passing of a companionship. At times, a youngster or high schooler may feel self-destructive because of specific life conditions that the individual probably shouldn't discuss, for example,

Having a mental problem, including gloom
Misfortune or struggle with dear companions or relatives
History of physical or sexual maltreatment
Issues with liquor or medications
Physical or clinical issues, for instance, becoming pregnant or having a physically communicated contamination
Being the survivor of tormenting
Being questionable of sexual direction
Perusing or hearing a record of self destruction or knowing a companion who kicked the bucket by self destruction
In the event that you have worries about a companion or relative, getting some information about self-destructive considerations and expectations is the most effective way to distinguish risk.

Murder and self destruction
In uncommon cases, individuals who are self-destructive are in danger of killing others and afterward themselves. Known as a manslaughter self

destruction or murder-self destruction, some gamble factors include:

History of contention with a mate or better half
Current family lawful or monetary issues
History of psychological well-being issues, especially gloom
Liquor or substance addiction
Approaching a gun
Beginning antidepressants and expanded self destruction risk
Most antidepressants are by and large protected, however the Food and Drug Administration expects that all antidepressants convey black box admonitions, the strictest alerts for remedies. Now and again, kids, teens and youthful grown-ups under 25 might have an expansion in self-destructive considerations or conduct while taking antidepressants, particularly in the initial not many weeks in the wake of beginning or when the portion is changed.

Nonetheless, remember that antidepressants are bound to lessen self destruction risk over the long haul by further developing mind-set.

High schooler self destruction counteraction

Connect — Preventing high schooler self destruction

Intricacies
Self-destructive contemplations and endeavored self destruction incur significant damage. For example, you might be so consumed by self-destructive contemplations that you can't work in your day to day routine. And keeping in mind that many endeavored suicides are rash demonstrations during a snapshot of emergency, they can leave you with long-lasting serious or extreme wounds, for example, organ disappointment or cerebrum harm.

For those abandoned after self destruction — individuals known as overcomers of self destruction — misery, outrage, sadness and culpability are normal.

Anticipation
To assist with holding yourself back from feeling self-destructive:

Seek the treatment you really want. In the event that you don't treat the hidden reason, your self-destructive considerations are probably going to return. You might feel humiliated to look for treatment for psychological wellness issues, however seeking the right treatment for sorrow, substance abuse or another hidden issue will help you have an improved outlook on life — and assist with protecting you.

Lay out your encouraging group of people. It might be difficult to discuss self-destructive sentiments, and your loved ones may not completely comprehend the reason why you feel the manner in which you do. Connect at any rate, and ensure individuals who care about you know what's happening and are there when you want them. You may likewise need to find support from your place of love, support gatherings or other local area assets. Feeling associated and upheld can assist with decreasing self destruction risk.

Keep in mind, self-destructive sentiments are transitory. In the event that you feel miserable or that everyday routine isn't worth experiencing any longer, recollect that treatment can assist you with recapturing your viewpoint — and life will improve.

Approach slowly and carefully and don't act indiscreetly.

Printed in Great Britain
by Amazon